Beauty Mark

Also by Suzanne Cleary

Trick Pear
Knowing Time

Suzanne Cleary

Winner of the John Ciardi Prize for Poetry
selected by Kevin Prufer

 BkMk Press
University of Missouri-Kansas City

BkMk Press
University of Missouri-Kansas City
5101 Rockhill Road
Kansas City, Missouri 64110
(816) 235-2558 www.umkc.edu/bkmk

Financial support for this project has been provided by the Missouri Arts Council,
a state agency.

Book Design: Susan L. Schurman
Author Photo: D. Langley
Managing Editor: Ben Furnish
Associate Editor: Michelle Boisseau
Executive Editor: Robert Stewart

BkMk Press wishes to thank Marie Mayhugh, Grace Stansbery, Zakiya Williams, and
Greyson Honaker.

Library of Congress Cataloging-in-Publication Data

Cleary, Suzanne.
  [Poems. Selections]
  Beauty Mark : Poems, winner of the John Ciardi Prize for Poetry, selected by Kevin Prufer /
Suzanne Cleary.
      pages cm.
  Includes bibliographical references and index.
  Summary: "The poems in this book use images and subjects drawn from 20th and 21st
century American popular culture to find transcendent meanings in the natures of beauty,
time, and, especially, art (including literature, music, visual art, dance, and food)"-- Provided
by publisher.
  John Ciardi Prize for Poetry
  ISBN 978-1-886157-92-7 (paperback : alk. paper)
  I. Title.
  PS3603.L4553A6 2013
  811'.6--dc23
                          2013034250

This book is set in Garamond Premier Pro and Minion Pro.

for Lou Winna Langley
and in memory of Ralph Langley

The imperfect is our paradise.
—Wallace Stevens

Acknowledgments

I thank each of the editors who welcomed my poems into journals and anthologies:

Best American Poetry 2009: "From *The Boy's Own Book...*"
BigCityLit.com: "Strong Bikini"
Caduceus: "Televangelists"
Connecticut Review: "Imagining the Shaker Meeting at Which the
    Founder Ann Lee Announces the Policy of Sexual Abstinence,"
    "Ring"
ConnotationPress.com: "Cezanne's Clogs," "Swimming with Miss Peggy
    Lee," "Freud's Little Statues"
Great River Review: "Asking for Breakfast," "Beauty Mark"
Margie: "As the Story Came Down to Me," "From The Boy's Own
    Book...," "Photograph Sent to the Widow Mary Todd Lincoln"
New Millennium Writings: "Let Me Reach for Outrageous Comparison"
Nimrod International Journal: "Amazing," "Italian Made Simple," (second-place
    winners of 2011 Pablo Neruda Prize for Poetry)
Ploughshares: "Temporary Tattoo"
Poetry Calendar 2009: "From *The Boy's Own Book...*"
Poetry Calendar 2010: "Running Backwards"
Poetry Calendar 2011: "Lines for the Actress Who Performed Shakespeare-in-the-
    Park With a Stick in Her Mouth"
Poetry International: "Polka"
Poetry London: "Pascal's Wager"
Riverine: An Anthology of Hudson Valley Writers: "Magnificent"
South85: "Into the Night," "Vic Damone"
Southern Poetry Review: "Cheese-of-the-Month Club," "In Memoriam,"
    "Running Backwards"

I also wish to thank the MacDowell Colony, Yaddo, and the Byrdcliffe Art Colony
for residencies during which I wrote many of these poems.

Beauty
Mark

FOREWORD

The other day, I was trying to draw a distinction between two very different kinds of poetic expression. The first group included poems that invite the reader into another mind, allowing us to experience it at work. These poems enact thought, creating the illusion of an often unsettled mind in motion. In the other group are poems that create the illusion of speech. Rhetorically sculpted, seemingly spoken directly to the reader, they're often inspired by a moment of realization that precedes their utterance; other times, insights are arrived at along the way, as if the speaker has stumbled upon them or talked herself into new awareness. If Dickinson is our American progenitor of the mind-in-motion poem, Whitman (and, more recently, McGrath, Halliday, Hoagland, and Duhamel) are poets of speech, conversation, pronouncement.

Suzanne Cleary is a poet of the second group, her poems frequently addressing the reader the way a friend might, someone quick with a story, a bit of advice, an observation of the world. "You could be a sin-eater," begins the poem "Hate Your Job? It Could Be Worse." "Enough about Cézanne's apples," declares another, "I, for one, am just as interested, / more interested, in Cézanne's clogs." Or, *What is beauty?* is a good question, but *What is a beauty mark?* / is equally good," begins a third.

What first fascinates me about Cleary's work is how it avoids the risks inherent here—for these plainspoken poems are not merely conversational, nor are they in any way simple. Beneath their amiable, glistening surfaces are deep concerns, for Cleary's true subjects are mortality, those qualities that define art, and our relationship to the divine. Although "Imagining the Shaker Meeting at Which the Founder Ann Lee Announces the Policy of Sexual Abstinence" begins with our speaker coyly recreating the scene—"How does a quiet room grow more quiet?" she asks with well-timed amusement. "It did."—the poem quickly reveals a truly complex engagement with the uncomfortable ways our worship brings us closer not merely to the divine, but to disconcerting self-knowledge. "She knew, I imagine," Cleary concludes,

> this moment was either
> the beginning of the end for the Shakers, or the beginning
> of her sect's immortality: an experiment so doomed
> no human could not identify with it.

Elsewhere, in "Italian Made Simple," Cleary tells us of a romance unfolding in the pages of a language textbook while the speaker truly—perhaps without even realizing it—communicates something of her loneliness and disconcerting pride. Or in "As the Story Came Down to Me," one of the most astonishing poems in the book, what appears to be a humorous story about the speaker's grandmother nearly being arrested for having too many plastic saint statues glued to her dashboard, becomes, instead, a poem about the creative process, about art and its origins in human empathy, the speaker abruptly announcing that she

> lied in saying it was my grandmother,
> although I did in fact see an old woman
> driving a dark blue Chevy with saints
> And I must confess I exaggerated the number of saints.
> I never saw a police car pull her over. I made that up.
> But I swear the short white-haired woman
> peering through the space between Joseph and Mary,
> I swear it brought tears to my eyes,
> and I am still trying to figure out how.

What drew me first to this manuscript may have been the easy confidence of Cleary's many voices, their adeptness with narrative, their skill with rhetoric, their concision of language and intriguing observations. For these, her poems—peopled with televangelists, the mischievous students of Rembrandt van Rijn, Sigmund Freud, and the apparition of Miss Peggy Lee—are already memorable. But they are not what made me select this book for the John Ciardi Prize. What delighted me on a second and third reading of *Beauty Mark* were the deeper currents here, the fine, complex psychological intelligence at work in these poems, the distances they invite me to leap between what these narrators tell me and what I find to be true in their stories. This is an ambitious, delightful, superior book, one I'm proud to have played a small part in bringing to readers.

—Kevin Prufer
Houston, Texas
2013

LINES FOR THE ACTRESS WHO PERFORMED SHAKESPEARE-IN-THE-PARK WITH A STICK IN HER MOUTH

What made you, that evening
      as you walked into Central Park, stop
          and stoop, pluck that stick from the grass,

and put it directly,
      without word or thought, into your mouth,
          clamp your teeth?

How did you know
      this was how to speak your lines that night:
          tongue pressed to rough-soft bark,

stick placed far back in your mouth
      so it pulled your lips taut, so you strained
          as if speaking for the first time?

Small woman holding like a terrier
      a stick in your mouth,
          you dared them to laugh,

the audience leaning forward, straining
      to understand what you said,
          until the difficult music of it

washed over them,
      washed them of desire
          for anything small as understanding.

It was *The Tempest*. You were Ariel—
      airy sprite, industrious servant,
          forty-year-old woman in green tights,

pressing the small stick into the role
      of the vast unspoken, the greater part
          of most that can be said.

You were not the one who said
    our little life is rounded with a sleep,
        but you had taken the very dirt

into your mouth, the stick clotted with earth.
    And you became a kind of blossom upon it,
        mortal, mortal, mortal.

IN MEMORIAM

Not a day goes by that you are not forgotten.
—"In Memoriam," *Binghamton Sun Bulletin*

Dear Jimmy, ten years since you left us
and not a day goes by that you are not forgotten.
When we open our eyes, we forget you.

When we open the newspaper, we forget you again.
We eat our toast burned to charcoal,
just the way you liked it, with a touch of butter

and the marmalade from Zalaffi's.
Sometimes we forget you when we wash the dishes, but
when we leave the dishes in the sink, we seldom forget you,

dear Jimmy. We seldom forget you when we laugh,
you whom we believe look down upon us each day,
you who promised to send us a sign

if you met God face to face,
but forgot to tell us what the sign would be,
and we forgot to ask.

Jimmy, in this morning's *Sun Bulletin*,
is this the sign: ambiguous construction, a possible
double-negative by the night editor, half asleep,

who grew distracted from her work by the moon,
startled by its steady, ordinary beauty?
Hardly a night goes by that she does not forget it,

or not not-forget it, but last night God tells her,
right? He says, *Stop. Just for a moment, stop.*
Look up. OK, he says this without words, Jimmy,

not that words are nothing he would say,
not that words are not useful, in their clumsy way.
It must be lonely for the editor, typing

in her office high above the traffic,
in the florescent light that makes time seem to
stand still, as if she will type this single

"In Memoriam" for all of eternity unless she stands,
moves from desk to fax to copy machine, performing
the small, necessary tasks that make a night pass.

She has a list of things not to forget.
The anniversary of your passing is on her list
because she did not know you, Jimmy,

except in that moment the moon
slipped out of the clouds,
and then, again, back behind them.

TEMPORARY TATTOO

Beside the cash register in my favorite used book store
I see a glass bowl of what seem to be postage stamps
until I look closer: temporary tattoos of red and green,

with ornate black lettering *Bruised Apple Books*.
Take one, says Andrew, *Take two*, as if he directs a film
about the struggle of an independent bookseller

and his ageing clientele, some of them tattooed
in the Summer of Love, some of them tattooed
by surgery, or time. I take one,

although I know a temporary tattoo
is oxymoronic, maybe just plain moronic,
something else the world does not need,

as no one needs the leather-bound collected Thackeray
or the first-edition *Joy of Sex* inscribed *Love,
from Guess Who?* A tattoo should be permanent,

a commitment, a cross-hatched cobra coiled
around the biceps, inks of deep blue and green
like the veins that pop from the carney's arm

when he makes a fist. A tattoo should not
smear, dissolve with baby-oil-on-tissue,
should be bold as a snake swallowing a mouse

and the mouse-shape traveling the length of it
like a bad idea shaping a life, distorting a life.
The apple is pink-red, like the tip of a cigarette,

its single leaf the green of the 1964 Chevy convertible
on cinder blocks behind the bookstore,
a car that will never run

despite the young man who works

under the hood every night until dark.
Someone should go to him and tell him

the sum is not always greater than its parts.
Sometimes the parts are what is valuable,
what can be parlayed into a life.

Tell him sell the tires, sell the wheels.
Tell him there is not enough light in all of his days
to spend evenings with his back to the stars,

staining his hands with grease and oil.
Someone should give him the tattoo
of the bruised apple, which will last

a week, at best. Tell him the Chevy's time
has come and gone, that nothing lasts forever
except our desire for things to last forever.

But he is too young to know this,
and nothing can convince him this is true.
Nothing written in any of these books

can show him what his strong hands
seem to show as they fold the oily rag
and drop the hood on another day

and in the gravel lot behind the bookstore
the last of the sun shines
pink, and everywhere, and always.

At first, it had seemed such a good idea,
>to open your home to the creamy, the crumbly,
the stinky, the blue, to open your home to this new life,
>the life where you open your mouth not to talk but to taste,
to find, the third Friday of every month, the box,
>heavy yet compact, its corrugated wings opening
onto another box, shiny and white, taped to its top
>a gold-edged card identifying the cheese by name and story,
to find at your door, dependably, a new reason
>to live in your body, to love your body:
the Venetian Pecorino, coated with black pepper
>*providing a distinct bite with a little heat,*
the Netherlands' Extra-Aged Farmer's Cheese, described as
>*the dairy world's equivalent of a Rembrandt or van Gogh,*
the description, true, sometimes a tad overripe, still,
>it seemed such a good idea to learn, to know, to savor
what at first you could barely discern, say,
>the Belgian goat cheese, *fruity, slightly herbed,*
its texture chalky yet creamy.
>What could this cheese not teach you
about contrast and balance, risk and poise?
>But now, each time you open the door, there is another cheese.
Now, Month Six, you doubt you can keep pace with it.
>It is likely to outrun you, even the cheese that is not runny,
even the aged cheese. You doubt your capacity for pleasure,
>your appetite for knowledge, your appetite itself. You doubt yourself worthy
of the gentle buffalo-milk cheese called Bishop's Blessing.
>And how, by the way, does a month pass so quickly?
Do not ask for whom the cheese tolls. It tolls for thee,
>in Pomfret, Vermont, where a raw-milk organic cheese ripens
in one of the few copper cheese vats in the United States,
>a vat that, given the chance, would sing like a steel drum,
call everyone in Pomfret out into the street
>to dance in a long, swaying line,
except that you doubt people dance in the street in Vermont,
>where, it is said, there are two seasons: winter and roadwork.
Maybe you should live in Vermont, where nights are long and cold,
>where the cheese is mostly local, and you doubt people say much about it.

You doubt anyone would approve
      of the gold-edged card that boasts of *the subtle nut flavor,*
its complex finish redolent of a cove north of Pomfret.
      Redolent, you turn the word over with your tongue, your mind.
Redolent of a cove is enough to make you sign on for another year,
      for isn't this what you want, what you have always wanted,
to bite into life so deeply you can taste where it began?
      Isn't that desire what brought you here, somewhere south of Pomfret?

tells the story of Mario and Marina,
      and by the end of Chapter 1, I've got it:
the *r* is a *d*, and Mario and Marina
      will fall in love, he an American
planning a business trip to Italy,
      she an Italian teaching English
in a school *in centro*, downtown,
      which I take to mean Wall Street,
maybe Tribeca or Nolita.
      For the first lesson, they meet
in Marina's *ufficio*, where they repeat
      the half-dozen Italian phrases for *hello*.
Both of them remain patient,
      cheerful, even, in the face of their task.
They name every single blessed thing
      on the desk. What good fortune it is
they cannot yet say, so many small things
      here before them: the pen, the paper, and
the pencil, too, the newspaper, the lamp.
      Marina pronounces each word slowly
while Mario watches her lips, repeats.
      What is this? Marina asks in Italian.
What is this? and Mario, under a spell,
      answers, although he cannot yet
be said to understand these words
      that are little more to him than sounds,
air blown through the shapes
      that Marina's lips make his lips make.
By Chapter 4, simple Italian leads Mario
      and Marina to the window, to the words
for *street, hospital, bicycle, child*,
      where simplicity threatens to abandon
these two people who are just trying
      to live, an idiomatic expression
for *to make money. No*, says Marina.
      That is not a child. That is not a girl.
a woman, a car, etcetera. Mario loves

the word *eccetera*, which he figures
will save him lots of time. When their time
        is up, Mario and Marina walk to the door,
at exactly the same moment say *la porta*.
        The next moment, they laugh. *Eccetera,*
eccetera. Because I cannot live
        in the simple present, where *Italian Made*
Simple begins, I read ahead.
        In Florence, on his business trip,
Mario buys for Marina a gold bracelet.
        A gold bracelet Mario buys for Marina.
Mario for Marina buys a gold bracelet.
        He does not yet understand that Marina
already knows that he loves her,
        that she has loved him since Chapter 5,
Familia, wherein Mario showed quick
        concern for her ill niece. Mario, alone
in Florence, on the far side of his voyage
        through the definite pronouns, the prepositions,
the baffling procession of possessive forms,
        Mario sits at a café, drinking
the beverage he ordered by mistake.
        When the waitress sets it brightly before him,
Piacere, Mario says, ever gracious.
        Mario, at the end of my textbook,
of your slow, sometimes laborious story,
        how will I live without you?
You do not yet know that the final lesson
        finds you and Marina deciding to marry,
to live in Rome, yet here, in Chapter 20,
        Firenze, still you sip and savor.
You open your dictionary.
        The small table at which you sit
is called *tavolino*, just as you had thought,
        and you smile to yourself,
now that you are lonely, now that you know
        you know by heart,
the meaning of every single blessed thing.

SILVER AMULET OF GANESHA,
THE ELELPHANT GOD

Elephant god the size of my thumbnail,
I could stare at the silver glob of you,
the gnarled and mottled blob of you, all day

and still I would fail to see the elephant trunk,
the stub legs folded into perfect lotus.
Protector of travelers, finder of lost objects,

it seems your journey has not been easy.
You were nearly lost: a slip of hand, of attention,
the silversmith held you too close to the flame

before scooping you up to the cooler air, saved.
I am told by the woman who sells you, *If your bus
crashes, Ganesha will save you from injury,*

and then I know, Ganesha, that I can nearly believe in you
for neither does my god stop the bus from crashing.
He too promises to save me, although not in this world.

Ganesha, I want to be saved in this world.
I think of the moment the silversmith
stared at you in your molten half-destruction,

your exquisite trunk and expressive mouth,
your fine East Indian ears, all run into one pool
of shimmering silver, your perfect form slipping

through itself toward the abstract.
Ganesha, what shifted inside of the silversmith
that she did not scrap you, start again? What

made her fashion for you this long and narrow trunk
that makes you look like a silver candle left burning all night?
Finder of lost objects, I imagine you looked at her

and your look said to her, *Enough. This is the god.*

And so you saved her, her journey ended.
Ganesha, I want to be saved in this world,

as the silversmith was saved when she stared at you
and she stopped, for a moment, her working, and she saw
the pure silver wreck of you wrought by the hand of flame.

MAGNIFICENT

In the grocery store parking lot there is
        a maroon station wagon with leopard seats,
above the front left wheel a patch of rust
        one could only call magnificent until one sees
the hood, studded with plastic tops from aerosol spray cans,
        each glued rim-down to the faded paint,
42 tops in all the known neons, black, white,
        and some colors for which there mercifully
are no names, for they would sound like *puce*.
        Whoever drives this car is shopping for groceries
and aerosol spray, or now standing in line choosing
        between Doublemint and miniature Chiclets,
no one you'd recognize as individualist, creative thinker,
        rabid consumer of ozone-destroying products—
hairspray, bug spray, foot spray,
        carpet cleaner, tile cleaner, oven cleaner,
although the car's floor does not suggest
        someone especially concerned with cleanliness:
candy wrappers, loose change, a torn and stained map
        from a trip long, long ago.
Whoever drives this car has seen many things,
        perhaps too many.
As she stands in line, she might reflect upon one of them
        except that she is not given to reflection,
believes it's not all it's cracked up to be, this business
        of the interior. She knows it's possible, after all,
to get carried away, to realize you can't let go.
        Before you know it, you drive your obsession everywhere.
Meanwhile, in the parking lot, a woman
        leans close to the maroon station wagon,
counting the number of plastic tops glued to the hood
        and she wants to believe it is changing her forever.
She knows there are chance encounters
        that can steer your life into another direction
or awaken inside of you the life gone dull, rusted.
        You can see something once and never be the same,
although you cannot will this, nor will it away.
        Magnificent, she thinks. *Bread*, she thinks.
Milk for tomorrow.

Swimming with Miss Peggy Lee

I am 50 years old and she is many years dead
        but we swim together in my college pool,
as together as possible for two lap-swimmers.
        I am focused almost entirely on that place inside of me
where I swim when the swimming goes well,
        until I notice her, some new woman, her stroke
stately, efficient, with a certain swing,
        her flutter kick powerful without being showy.
She is slower than I but has more stamina.
        As I rest, goggles on forehead, I watch her flip
heels over head, push off from the wall, and glide
        as if slipping into a tight sequined gown, letting it fall
over her head and shoulders, shimmying it down
        over her hips, and it hits me: *The Ed Sullivan Show*,
1966, my grandmother pointing at the little screen,
        That's Miss Peggy Lee, who, in truth, scared me
with her platinum hair like sheet metal, her beauty mark.
        Her dark eyes looked sideways as she sang,
as if she heard a different song
        from the song we heard her sing.
But today, behind her goggles, I think she stares
        straight ahead, and I think her beauty mark
has washed away, or fallen off in the pool.
        Maybe it's stuck to my foot, or,
as someone showers, it swirls down the drain.
        I asked my grandmother, *What's that black dot?*
even then my attention drawn to the small, the incidental,
        making of it a still center around which everything moves,
like the round mouth of Miss Peggy Lee as she comes up for air.
        Her stroke looks effortless, as if she could swim forever.
She was famous for practicing until her band nearly collapsed,
        and then she'd say, *One more time. From the top.*
My dreams are not usually this long, nor are my poems,
        but I feel Miss Peggy Lee has something to teach me
and I have not yet learned it, even identified it.
        I feel sheepish for having imagined
her beauty mark stuck to my foot,

which now seems disrespectful, and not as funny
as I thought it would be. Resting, winded,
        my elbows on the side of the pool, I wonder
how she developed a form that fits her so perfectly
        she can forget it, disappear inside of it,
inside of herself, this her true element, it seems,
        as she cups her hands and pulls the water toward her,
    as if to say, *Reach, Darlin'. Just reach,*
        and it'll be alright.

CÉZANNE'S CLOGS

Enough about Cézanne's apples. I, for one,
        am just as interested, more interested,
in Cézanne's clogs, thick gray leather
        with closed heels, like leather gravy boats,
although they're hard to see in this photograph,
        Cézanne standing in a small pile of leaves
in what looks to be an apple orchard,
        his right hand lifted, resting on a branch.
His left hand rests on his hip, lightly,
        as if he were about to reach into his pocket
when someone asks, *Would you mind, Monsieur,*
        if I took your photograph? and Cézanne,
instead of unfurling a large white handkerchief,
        freezes. He looks straight into the camera,
looks uncomfortable despite the inspiration
        to pose with his hand thrown over
the tree branch. Only his feet look comfortable,
        in the putty-colored, paint-spattered clogs
so supportive he can stand for hours
        in front of his several easels, strolling casually,
and as if casually, from one canvas to the next,
        following the light, following the brush.
Wearing these clogs Cézanne could forget his feet,
        and if you can forget your feet you can forget
your entire body, can't you, for hours on end?
        You become lighter, then, light itself.
Maybe in front of his easel Cézanne eventually
        grew thirsty, drank coffee, grew hungry,
ate the apple most soft, most mottled,
        but I doubt that Cézanne,
in these clogs, had need to sit, unless to see
        his canvas from another angle, or to wait out
daylight's slow walk. These storm-cloud-colored clogs,
        these driftwood-at-twilight-colored clogs,
scuffed and dusty, held together by nails and by gum,
        these have yet to be studied by art historians.

I propose a symposium on these clogs
        that led Cézanne out of his studio
and then led him back,
        and each night stood beside the painter's bed
like two dreams waiting to be dreamt.

POSTCARD FROM THE ART COLONY

Consider this: anything can become a poem
if arranged into lines, anything, as long
as there is, behind the lines, a confidence, a willingness
to reconsider. People who work at Yaddo, I mean who live in town,
soon after dawn drive up the long hill. They walk through the mansion
carrying baskets of bedsheets. A young woman sits cross-legged
at the top of the grand staircase, polishing each spindle
with a spray-bottle of bright blue fluid, a small cloth.
This morning, outside my study window, a project:
the long-needle pine needs pruning. When I go to my desk,
I discover a ladder propped against the tree,
but no one in sight, as if this is all that is necessary:
choosing the tree, and the ladder,
and leaning them against each other.

STRONG BIKINI

after misreading a resort-wear advertisement

Three turquoise triangles
    sheening and sheer, stretched
        taut against the taut roundnesses of her,

two pieces strung to each other
    by silk ties,
        the third piece strung to itself

by silk ties, knotted
    as if to hold the boat to shore,
        the little knots press into the skin

as if to test,
    Can it be real,
        such youth and beauty?

Strong bikini, that dares
    to ask the question,
        to strain for the answer,

strong bikini, that takes our thoughts
    and holds and slightly lifts them,
        our thoughts.

is the last place one expects to find
a lock of hair, blond, golden as if the sun shone on it
yesterday, not 100 years ago, 1907, when the book's
dark green linen cover shone bright as the thick grass

upon which a young woman sits, reads
Penmanship, Postal Cards, Telegraphing, then
turns to the chapter entitled *The Personal Note*,
twirling this hair around her finger, lingering

over two paragraphs, *Of Friendship*, and *Of Affection*:
"Letters of friendship perpetuate the ties of regard
of those who are absent from each other. The chief charm
of a letter of friendship is its natural, conversational style."

"Letters of affection are as varied as our relations to others
are varied, and may be simply the expression of kindly feeling,
or may be dictated by the strongest impulses
that move the human heart."

The young woman studies the distinction
between friendship and affection,
between what she dare and dare not write,
in 1907, but it could be any year, couldn't it, Dearest Friend?

Can you not, My Partner in Imagining, place yourself
in the position of this young woman?
Is it not, for you as for me, the swiftest of leaps
to suppose the woman writes the note, then

tears it to shreds, and, then, there she sits,
in the bright grass, with the lock of hair in her hand, and
no way to reattach it, and nowhere to, quickly,
before anyone sees her, hide it, so no one will know

the improper correspondence between her behavior and decorum?
Please forgive my possible indelicacy in painting this scene

as though it play before your eyes as it does before mine,
as also, in advance, I beg your pardon

for writing that I lifted the hair close to my face.
My lips nearly brushed it, that I might find there
the scent of summer grass, finding, instead,
a faint smell of dust. My Absent Friend, if I know you at all,

I know you smile as I hesitate, my pen in hand.
Dust always dances in sunlight. Is that not your thought?
I await your word as to whether this particular dust
rises from a dirt road on which a horseman pass by.

All I can know, just now, is that the woman tied the hair
with a blue ribbon gone gray, dulled with time as the hair is not,
the hair preserved in *The Manual of Proper Correspondence*, perfectly,
as if—permit me this indulgence—

the rules in this thin volume protect us
from time, as from ourselves. Will you allow me this conceit?
The imagination cannot do other than seek
correspondence, proper or otherwise. I draw comparison

so as to find the right relation, the proper correspondence,
as today, My Best Reader, I found a book
from which fell a lock of hair, unlocking
thought of you, Dear Poem.

Exercises from the *Manual of Proper Correspondence*, 1889

I.
Write a letter from a summer resort to a friend, urging him to join you. Describe the attractions.

II.
Write a letter of recommendation for Mr. Johnson L. Hibbard, who has very acceptably occupied the position of foreman in your wheel works for some time. State that you would be glad to retain him in your service, but that he has decided to go west.

III.
Write a letter to a friend who has had his home, representing the savings of many years, destroyed by fire, barely escaping with his family, and losing valuable relics and souvenirs which money cannot replace. Assure him of your sympathy.

IV.
Write a letter to a friend who has received serious injuries in a railroad collision, compelling the amputation of a limb. Try to comprehend the situation in which he is so sadly and suddenly placed; let your thoughts be active, and anticipate, if possible, his anxieties for the future.

Make your letter cheery and hopeful, and write at least three or four pages, remembering that he has time to read or listen to just such letters while lying upon his couch day after day.

TELEVANGELISTS

I won't say all of them, but almost
all of them shout as if standing in the shower,
eyes closed, leaning slightly forward, hands out

as if reaching for soap, for towel,
almost all of them straining their voices
as they stand under the roaring shower of God's love,

which they believe also falls on us who listen
or perhaps just stare. There is, after all,
so much to see: the sparkly clothes,

the wild hair lifted and lacquered into rapture,
the jewelry from cuff links to earrings
glaring in the studio lights

as glare the gold brocade armchairs with gilt armrests,
dear God, a tempest of waste, of bad taste.
I wonder about this worldly display.

Does God love it? forgive it?
Love-and-forgiveness is God's specialty, say the televangelists,
who do not care what we think of them.

It is not our judgment they fear.
What is it to live as they do?
I don't mean the clothes, the cameras.

I mean, what is it to love
something so much you will shout about it,
you will stand up and speak, and soon

your body keen with it, a love so great
you know it does not come from yourself?
I wonder what it is to surrender.

How does it feel when the wardrobe assistant says,

We need these shoulder pads a little bit bigger,
and you slip off your jacket, just hand it over,

or when Make-Up arrives with more blue eye shadow
and you bow your head as if in prayer?
It is hard for me to believe God loves the televangelists

except in their quiet moments, just before the broadcast,
accepting the last spritz of hairspray and touch of powder,
the silk handkerchief tweaked into the breast pocket.

When the *Applause* sign lights, I believe God must clap
his hands over his ears. He must lean forward
in his rocker and turn down the volume,

even as He sits in each seat in the studio audience
and in each of the cars in a traffic jam outside the studio,
cabbies honking their horns to kingdom come.

God is everywhere, the televangelists know, and they are certain
as they raise their jeweled hands and open their mouths to shout,
this is the problem with God: He is everywhere

and so we are blind to Him, and deaf.

God Visits the Televangelists

God loves the moments backstage,
before the broadcast,
the televangelists taking deep breaths
so they will be able to shout and sing,
televangelists tucking handkerchiefs into their cuffs
so they will be ready for the sweat and the tears.
God walks among them undetected
as they make the small adjustments
a human body requires.

God loves the moment when everything on set
goes quiet and dark. It reminds Him of the first day,
early morning, just before He created light,
before He had thought of animals
or any of the sounds that animals make.

On the dark set God can barely see,
but of course He can see: the televangelists
stand in a circle, their hands joined, heads bowed.
God can barely hear their hushed voices,
but of course he knows what they say.

Is it a true visit if God does not speak,
if the televangelists do not feel his presence
as He sits on a metal folding chair
to the side of the sandwich cart?
Why has God come here if not to speak,
especially with the televangelists so eager to hear?

When the televangelists drop their hands
a handkerchief falls to the floor,
but God does not pick it up.
How does God choose what to do,
and what not to do? This is a question
the televangelists frequently ask, attempt to answer,

but not at this moment, when a red bulb flashes,
a man in a baseball cap raises his hand,

fingers counting *5, 4, 3...*

God loves this count-down, time
his favorite of all his creations
for it contains all else, each for its time.
God takes a sip of his coffee,
tilts his chair back on two legs.
God loves to enter time. It needn't be here,
with the televangelists, but today it is,
this late-morning broadcast, live.

Live! a voice announces, lights blaze
from ceiling and floor all at once.
How do they do that? God wonders,
for knowledge does not preclude wonder,
not in Heaven and not, sometimes, on earth.

God listens to the televangelists as he drinks his coffee,
but soon finds himself remembering
the first morning with animals,
some of them silent, awaiting their voices,
some of them calling with their original calls,
the bear clucking, the horse cooing, the worm
singing, for its brief hour, the flute-like descending spiral
God would give to the vireo. *Oh,*

those were the days, God sighs,
for on earth there is nostalgia, inextricable from time.
Already God is longing for that moment
the handkerchief fell from the cuff of the televangelist—
not so he himself could pick it up, tuck it back into place,

but so again he could savor
the imperfection that visits each human moment,
this too God's creation, imperfection and the idea of imperfection,
the inner world as well as the outer world.

God loves the moment when the one televangelist
feels her handkerchief slip, and fall, and another televangelist
hesitates before giving her his own handkerchief,
and then they walk together into the light.
God loves the hesitation most of all

for it is most human. God loves most of all
he who does not easily welcome Him, but does.
God loves the coffee and even the metal folding chair
which, understandably, no one loves,
but God takes a deep breath, now, and he stands.

For reasons beyond human understanding,
it is time for God to leave. It is past time
for God to leave, and he has left,
his visit complete as any earthly thing.

PASCAL'S WAGER

Pascal's Wager is the kind of thing
you would discuss with a beer in your hand,
but then there was always a beer

in one of your hands, or passing from one to the other,
that summer we talked on your porch,
those rainy upstate nights, hot pavement steaming

as it cooled, the steam like fog close over a river,
beginning to lift toward invisibility.
I remember the wager like this: if we believe in God,

there is at least a chance we will see Heaven,
whereas, if we do not believe, we forfeit our place
in paradise. Pascal wrote there is no harm

in believing. If it turns out there is no God,
we've lost, he said, nothing, and if we do not believe,
and it turns out we are right, we have gained nothing,

Pascal not the kind of person, evidently,
to take satisfaction in having been right,
damned but right. I knew you drank. I saw the bottles.

I sat in your kitchen and I saw them, beside the stove.
You set your beer down to take a pot from the cupboard,
to pour rice into boiling water. You set it down again

to briefly admire, then chop, carrots and ginger,
to rinse red grapes, place them in a bowl,
all the while the two of us talking, a feast of ideas

and easy silence, as the small kitchen filled
with the smells of earth and, for all we knew,
for all we know, Heaven. When I think of you,

years later, it is usually because there is something
I want to tell you, or there is something I wonder about,
and I am alone in my wonder. I have thought

memory both Heaven and Hell. I wonder
if it is the same for you. Pascal's theology,
as I understand it, examines doubt

because he believes faith commodious beyond reason,
as is God, who has made earth our home,
and lets us mistake it for Heaven.

THE GLASS HALF FULL

If the glass is half full,
its full is not entire.
It lacks what fullness requires.

If the glass is half empty,
its emptiness pales.
It carries what fullness entails.

POLKA

Dancing the polka is like walking
       on a ship's deck
during a storm, water flying into the air,
       sliding in sheets across the gray
wood. Each time the ship
       tilts, you take two hop-like
steps in one direction, and
       then, determined to
keep walking, keep your balance,
       you, with the next wave, hop-skip
another direction. The ocean spray
       blinds you. It ruins your best clothes.
There is someone in your arms, and this is what
       makes it a polka, although she or he
does not look into your eyes, and you
       do not look, either, at your partner,
which would be the waltz, or the tango, which
       you will not dance this side of Heaven,
although to dance the polka is definitely
       to think of death, your partner's shoulder
surprisingly small in your hand. With
       your other hand, you hold aloft
your partner's hand and, arms outstretched,
       the two of you are almost like
the prow of a great ship, those carved,
       streaming-haired, fierce-faced
angels that stare out to sea,
       except the image of that prow, any prow,
too dramatic for you. Drama embarrasses
       anyone who has learned the polka
from grandparents, whose grandparents
       learned it from their grandparents, who left
Petrovavest for Bratislava, Bratislava
       for Prague, for ships that took six days
and five nights to cross the ocean.
       They never spoke of the crossing,
not even to each other. Likely, they knew
       that *polka* is from the Czech for "half-step,"

pulka a rapid shift from one foot to the other,
　　　　the basic step of the polka: a starting
and, immediately, a hesitation
　　　　before plunging into the moment
with this person who is in your arms.
　　　　You might as well call the dance
Walking the Ship Deck During a Storm
　　　　that Partly—Holy Mother, Forgive Me—
I Did Not Want to Survive, this dance
　　　　that could more succinctly be known as
Long Marriage, although you
　　　　who were raised on the polka would never
say this, speak of this, this
　　　　rush and near-collapse, over
and over again, this
　　　　two hop-steps this way, two hop-steps that.
God. You're beautiful when your hair is wet.

Imagining the Shaker Meeting at which the founder Ann Lee Announces the Policy of Sexual Abstinence

However long the agenda that evening,
however few the refreshments, late the hour,
it is not hard to imagine that when Ann Lee declared

her sect would abstain from all sexual relations,
she got their attention, one and all,
from the farm boys glad to be indoors, and sitting,

to the elderly women nodding over their sewing baskets.
Sexual abstinence. I am sure she repeated the announcement,
if not exactly in these words.

How does a quiet room grow more quiet?
It did. Maybe there was a little cough
from someone who had just taken a sip of tea, but

mostly there was a silence found only inside of tree trunks,
and it lasted through Ann Lee's explanation:
sexual abstinence is required because Shakers believe in no pleasure

that cannot be shared by all.
Then, all shared silence for a full minute.
Likely there was little pleasure in it.

It is not hard to imagine the Shakers, at first, afraid
to look at each other, all of them
staring down into their laps

or at the floor's hand-planed pine boards, set
so smoothly against one another they seemed of one piece.
Who was the first to shift buttocks on the smooth maple bench?

Who was the first to think, *Might not
sexual pleasure be shared among all of us?
Could we not, Mother Lee, form a committee?*

Standing on the dais at the front of the meeting hall,
Ann Lee looked long and hard at her flock,
at the table at the back of the room littered

with paper napkins and Styrofoam cups
and the last, hard bagels,
and she knew, I imagine, this moment was either

the beginning of the end for the Shakers, or the beginning
of her sect's immortality: an experiment so doomed
no human could not identify with it.

Hate your Job? It Could Be Worse.

You could be a sin-eater. You could live in the Middle Ages
in Wales or France or Italy, primarily,
live at the edge of the village, alone

because of your job: When someone dies, it's up to you
to take the sin from his body so he can enter Heaven
without waiting, without the inconvenience of more prayer.

Instead of selling cars or parking cars, instead of treating cancer,
or teaching English as a Second Language,
instead of adding numbers or eliminating pests,

you could be the one who stands before the body,
places on its chest a little salt, a crust of bread.
Then, you eat.

Someone gives you a coin, a small cup of beer or milk
to wash the sin down. With your luck, true, you would be the sin-eater
who gets milk instead of beer, and it would be warm milk,

watery, slightly blue. Silent, people stare
as you wipe your mouth on the back of your hand,
stare as you, bearer of sin after sin, turn, walk away.

To get back to your cave, far from the village,
you could walk for hours, wishing that something
would lift you up out of your body, as the sin lifted

through the dead man's chest, drawn irresistibly to the bread,
and once the sin was lifted, the soul itself, grown light, could rise.
Walking through the dark, you would give your soul

for a desk job, give your soul to be the teenager
standing ten feet from the jackhammers,
holding in one hand a cigarette, in the other hand an orange flag.

The boy's orange flag is a beautiful thing

reflected in the shine on a new black Mercedes.
It could be worse. He could live in the Middle Ages.

You could live in the Middle Ages,
when there was ignorance
and injustice.

LAMENT

after "Threnody," by Cleve Gray

To place your hands on the top edge of lament,
      you must climb a ladder.

To press your forehead to the lowest reach of lament,
      you must lie on your stomach.

To stretch your arms wide enough to embrace lament,
      this is not possible in a human body.

Lament is a dark canvas that covers four walls,
      a room-within-the-room, a room with no doors

save tall figures of gray and deep red.
      To call the figures *doors* requires you to leap

with your poor, human mind—as these figures leapt
      from the painter's memory of an ancient Greek statue:

the ideal body, that does not exist as flesh and blood,
      a body that cannot bleed except

figuratively, into more thought.
      To think, as the painter thought, of the war dead,

you must close your eyes and press your palms together.
      One palm is the living, one palm the dead.

One body, you must think,
      and that body, somehow, a door.

HOLY WATER

At Easter every year
the priest poured a small vial of it
for each family in the parish

my grandmother pouring hers
into a silvery-blue font
inside her bedroom door

a little pocket of Heaven
into which she dipped her hand
each time she entered the room

touching just her fingertips
to the ordinary water
blessed by the priest

and surely blessed also
by my grandmother
as she took the water

to her forehead and to her heart
and then to each shoulder
of her plaid housedress

then pressed her fingertips
to her mouth
for a quick kiss

never stopping, never breaking her stride
as she balanced a pile of folded towels
or swept my grandfather's slippers

to their place beside the bed,
or gave me the fancy hairbrush
she kept on top of the bureau

my grandmother never wondering, it seemed,
what miracle had transpired
to make the water holy

perhaps her wonder taken entirely
by the powdery smell of the towels
or the clean scent of my hair

but that would be to doubt
the capacity of my grandmother
for wonder, for love,

for love and wonder are the same thing,
what the priest felt, I believe,
as he held his hands above the water

and felt the transformation
from the tips of his fingers
and all down his arms

as the water changed God
into something close, and ordinary,
and simple, and here.

Scene Hand-Painted on a Skirt

It is a generic palm tree,
      generic stretch of beach,
            but, behind the tree,

there is a smear of orange cloud
      that streams like a banner tossed by seawind,
            tossed and twisted and tousled by wind,

not because the skirt flutters
      on a branch at the flea market,
            but because the orange paint

flares and falters, flames
      in an imaginary wind,
            brisk and salt, this

not because the painter's eye,
      the painter's hand, amateur,
            did more than love the cotton,

pale blue, tissue-thin,
      than love the idea of orange,
            of orange against blue—

but because the cloud,
      well-loved but generic, the cloud,
            through a combination

of hard wear and washing,
      drifted, as from decoration to consequence,
            poured into itself, and through.

DENISE POIRET

Denise Poiret's stockings were the colors of jelly,
raspberry, blackberry, shiny silk chosen to show off
her thin ankles, the bright dresses her husband made for her,

loose frocks with flat pleats, wide-collared coats
embroidered with silver threads, with gold,
Denise his best manikin, still slight

after five children, girls with her dark hair,
Denise who could tie a piano scarf around her waist
and so would the other women in Paris,

Denise a painting wherever she stood,
who knew, without ever being taught,
how to make an entrance: pause

in the doorway, just stand there,
one foot slightly before the other,
feet turned slightly outward, before stepping in.

How does one do it, live for beauty?
In Richmond, Virginia, there is a mansion
where no one lives except as stories

of Before the War Between the States,
a world of prepositions, on the poster bed
a dress of white lawn waiting for the mistress

having her hair combed, arranged atop her head,
downstairs, on the 12-foot dining table, walnut
with inlay of bird's-eye maple,

a set of china waiting for breakfast,
upon each fruit plate a painting of a fruit,
a different fruit for each plate, such that one imagines

children happily arguing for the peach,

or the plum, or the lemon, or the cherry,
china so fine it is, held to light, translucent,
the painting so lifelike it includes fruit flies,
on the fruit itself or on the milky background,
as if the painter thought to perfect the painting

by adding imperfection to the scene.
How does one live with art? Does art set the table
for beauty, who may or may not dine?

Does fancy set the table for art, real flies swarming
at each plate as the smell of cornbread rises up
from the servants' kitchen, below, unseen?

Paul Poiret spread carpets upon the lawn,
invited friends and strangers to a costume ball,
with wine and fruit kept cool by an ice dolphin

afloat on its own melting.
Denise wore a gold turban and green tunic,
gold shoes that looked ready to grant wishes,

as she stood in the doorway, looking out,
ten years before she would walk away
from all this, whatever it was.

THE ARMS OF THE VENUS DE MILO

Close analysis of the musculature of the famous Venus de Milo--the ancient Greek statue
of Aphrodite found on the island of Melos in 1820--shows that she couldn't hold on to her
drapery even before the statue lost its arms. —Elizabeth Wayland Barber
Women's Work: The First 20,000 Years

The myth is that we do not think of her arms, we do not miss them
due to the spell, the spill, of her torso with its perfect compact breasts,
the full basin of her pelvis, tipped, one hip slipped free
of drapery dripping like candle wax over what we know of her legs,
which are both sturdy and graceful, one foot accepting her full weight
so the other may touch the ground as a lion or deer touches the ground,
lightly, the Venus de Milo a marvel of grace, of balance, even without arms,
although the weight of their absence pulls us, those who believe that in one arm
she holds a shield, in the other arm a mirror with which to admire her own beauty,
and those who contend that the Venus de Milo in fact spins thread,
the *musculature of what is left* congruent with the Greek manner of spinning:
the left arm raised, hand even with head, holding sheep's wool
from which a drop-spindle dangles, spinning, at the knees.
Right arm folded across her waist, Venus guides the wool into thread,
thumb and middle finger twisting the fibers into one
until the thread grows so long that the spindle
touches the ground, stops. Venus bends,
winds the thread, resumes.
But now, as she has come to us, her spindle
spins freely, as if it will never stop.
Venus de Milo stares off into space
as she works. She is nude,
the better to work.

From *The Boy's Own Book:*
A Complete Encyclopedia of all the Diversions Athletic, Scientific, and Recreative, of Boyhood and Youth by William Clarke

William Clarke would have us believe
time rests lightly on the boy of 1829,
light as a penny placed atop the hand,

the hand pulled suddenly out, and turned
so as to catch the penny
before it hits the ground,

a trick with nearly endless
variations: penny placed on the forehead,
the elbow, the knee, *etcetera*.

Gravity is a game to the boy of 1829,
even as he learns to chop wood,
to shoot birds out of the sky.

The weight of his own body
may provide him hours of delight,
as in jumping over a trench,

vaulting over a wooden horse,
or performing what William Clarke names
The Deep Leap, wherein the boy stands

on a flight of stairs, jumps
clear to the floor. Clarke adds, *We do not, however,
much approve of this exercise,*

in his 300-page compendium this comment
a rare appearance of Clarke's own voice,
such that from this point forward

one boy understands Clarke's silence as tacit approval
of the tricks involving fire or knives or even glass,
which is dear and likely to shatter

if instructions are not followed
precisely, this boy most likely a bookworm
interested in *Card Tricks, Arithmetical Dazzlers,*

the thick chapter *Riddles and Puns,*
wherein words shift shape
like smoke relighting the candle.

This is the boy who will grow
to be the tallest man in the county
while his daredevil brother, come spring,
will take the fever, and die.

Why is a pack of cards like a garden?
Why is sealing wax like a soldier?
Why is a man like a burning candle?

What is the weight of the moon?

PHOTOGRAPH SENT TO THE
WIDOW MARY TODD LINCOLN

By training and temperament, the photographer
can lift light from darkness, and so he can bend,
for hours, over glass plates and emulsions,
can hang print after print on strings across the darkroom,

say *No, no*, without losing hope,
until the night he perfects it:
an improvement upon, he believes,
Mary Todd Lincoln's favorite photograph of herself:

alone in her sewing room, where she sits,
hands folded, in the high-backed chair,
her face unaccountably oval,
her thick body almost lovely, draped

in heavy satin of deep red.
If someone asked her why she preferred this photograph
among all of other others, she would lie,
It was my favorite dress, an excess of modesty

in a life full of excess, lately a sorrow so heavy
there are days she does not leave her bed,
while the photographer finds a way,
through the manipulation of negatives,

to make the husband, dead three years Saturday,
stand behind the chair, husband and wife together
in the room where he seldom appeared.
I pray, writes the photographer, *you will find comfort*

in this small token of my art.
How could he have seen? Accustomed to gradations
of light and line, how could he have imagined
the widow's wild screams, her terror at seeing

her husband's ghost, and close at her shoulder?
As long as he had stared at the woman's folded hands,

adjusted their paleness against the dark satin,
how could the photographer have imagined her

throwing her hands into the air,
beating the air with her fists?

Playing the Famous Trick

No one knows exactly how or why
or even if, but the story persists,
for who does not want to imagine Rembrandt's studio?

A washerwoman dressed as the Virgin Mary drinks a cup of beer
while John the Baptist plays cards with Jesus,
the room crowded with easels and plaster casts,

Rembrandt's students moving from canvas to canvas,
from their own paintings to that of the master.
Who does not want to imagine Rembrandt's great portraits

half-finished, the eyes wrong, or the nose, maybe
sunlight streaming from two directions at once, its source unresolved?
Imagine Rembrandt's self-portrait of 1631

before the brown velvet hat sports the magnificent white feather.
Who doesn't want to be tickled by that feather-shaped darkness?
Imagine the students playing the famous trick on their teacher:

painting life-size guilders on the studio floor,
then watching to see if Rembrandt pauses,
if Rembrandt bends to pick up the coins.

Over months, one at a time the guilders would appear,
so the story goes, each coin the work of only one student,
for this was a contest for anyone brave enough to risk

the master's wrath—his rage at being duped, at looking ridiculous,
his greater rage when the coin looked ridiculous,
too dull or too shiny, too flat.

Sometimes, to freshen the trick, someone sacrifices a real coin.
Imagine that. Imagine a thread
tied to the coin.

In the story, Rembrandt never catches on to the trick,
always pauses at the painted coin, thus

sketching and resketching this lesson in the studio's
charcoal-dust-and-paint-fumed air: a portrait of Rembrandt
showing his students that an artist must risk everything,
must be at the same time both stupid and brilliant,

Rembrandt's trick this stopping in his tracks, and looking,
eyes quizzical then bright, smile faint then widening
as he watches his students watching him,

watching him bend toward the coin,
seeing the master play the fool,
the greatest fool of all.

As the Story Came Down to Me

My grandmother was arrested
      nearly, for driving with too many saints on her dashboard,
the officer insisting that the nine plaster statues
      obstructed her view, violated some law
in our Catholic-thick town.
      A moving violation is the most serious kind,
beyond the purview of saints Joseph or Dominic, or even Jude,
      and Saint Christopher, Patron Saint of Travelers, was here
the chief offender for, as you know, he carries the Christ child
      on his shoulder, and so it was probably Christ's head,
that particular statue, that broke the camel's back.
      The officer was a good and gentle man,
as the story came down to me.
      He let my grandmother off with a warning
to prune the dash of six or seven saints.
      Ask someone to help you pry them loose, he offered.
We wouldn't want any to break.
      Just doing his job, an honest man, more honest
than I, who have lied in saying it was my grandmother,
      although I did in fact see an old woman
driving a dark blue Chevy with saints.
      And I must confess I exaggerated the number of saints.
I never saw a police car pull her over. I made that up.
      But I swear the short white-haired woman
peering through the space between Joseph and Mary,
      I swear it brought tears to my eyes,
and I am still trying to figure out how.

VIC DAMONE

I said *Vic Damone.* He was a singer, like Mike Douglas
or Jerry Vale or Steve Lawrence. Think narrow tie
and pastel shirt, a pleasant enough face, pleasant enough voice

singing the standards, the love songs of his parents' courtship.
Think singing new songs so that they sound old, wrong,
nothing to fall in love by, but Vic Damone a star

in my family's firmament because of the famous elevator ride.
At the Jersey shore for our summer vacation,
in a hotel with an outdoor pool, it was the afternoon

my sister and I were allowed to sunbathe by ourselves
as we waited for my mother to come down,
as my father took a nap in the room.

Could it have been that my mother and father
both took a nap, together? This question did not occur to me.
Anyway, we dangled our feet in the water, made slappy,

sloppy footprints to the plastic lawn chairs, and we waited.
When my mother stepped into the elevator, there he was,
Vic Damone, like any man wearing a polo shirt and plaid shorts.

My mother, bright white towels
pressed to her pink bathing suit with the boy-cut legs,
my mother smelled of suntan oil, and did not speak a word

to Vic Damone, did not even look at him, just at his reflection,
which she could not help but see in the silver doors
until the doors slid open onto sunlight. She walked over to us

and sat, began combing my sister's hair into a pony tail
while Vic Damone paused beside the elevator.
He put on his sunglasses, lit a cigarette,

maybe preparing to meet his agent or sign a contract,
to be driven to a rehearsal for a show. Then he turned,

headed into the lobby, and my mother, still combing, whispered,

That's Vic Damone, as if she spoke not a man's name, but,
rather, a verb or noun, and she was enriching our vocabulary,
vicdamone meaning "to prepare for departure" or "to pause, reconsider,"

or *vicdamone* meaning "privacy in a public space,"
vicdamone the discretion that keeps strangers from saying
what could distract them from other, more important, things.

The Navigator

My father-in-law, thirty years an airline navigator

      in the days of compass and slide rule, loved

to tell of the pilot who always set his coffee cup

      on top of the navigator's map,

the navigator always asking the pilot to please

      remove the cup, out of respect for the map,

if not for him, as well as for practical reasons.

      This one day, one leg of a routine flight,

it happened again: the pilot set his cup on the map. Here,

      my father-in-law, ace navigator

of story as of airplane, would pause.

      Well, he would say,

the navigator checked the fuel gauges, consulted the atlas,

      calculated something on his clipboard.

After they landed, the pilot reviewed the logbook, asked

      why the flight had taken an hour longer than usual.

Wind, said the navigator, as the pilot understood

      they had flown around the cup.

AMAZING

Amazing the number of people who, on learning
       that you live on Elm Street, make a joke about the movie.
           Amazing, too, the delight they find in their own wit

so contagious that you, almost always, have to laugh along with them,
       this circumstance surely a piece of Heaven fallen to earth,
           although little do these people know that the nightmare,

the real nightmare, happened on Pine Street, the corner of Pine Street
       and Elm, one day six years ago, when Patty, home early
           from her shift at the hospital, pulled up

in front of her house, 5 Pine, and decided
       to walk to the Elm Street Deli, for a pack of cigarettes.
           Behind the counter, Andre was watching the TV

tuned to his favorite investment program, *today's*
       best opportunity blaring past the pegboard display
           of aspirin and eyeglass repair kits. Andre nodded to the TV

as he handed Patty her change, saying, *I'm retiring early, Pat,*
       and Patty shot back, *Yeah, me too. I'm beat.*
           So far so good. Until Patty, half way across the street,

ready to light up, saw her car: roof crushed,
       windshield cracked into approximately
           a million pieces held together by some law of physics

11th graders know for two weeks. And so Patty ran back
       for Andre, the two of them ending up at the front fender,
           speechless. Andre noticed the pine-scented cardboard tree

still dangling from the rear-view mirror. Andre noticed details.
       You can't own a deli a block from a high school
           and not notice details: soda can up the sleeve, bagel

down the pants, beef jerky down the pants.
       Andre noticed, at the car's front left wheel,

a rock the size of a softball, but reddish and rough.

It was as hot as toast from Hell. Andre, always quick, ready
        for any opportunity, had touched the rock,
                briefly. *Yikes*, he said, *Holy shit! Do you know what this*

is, Pat? A meteor. Then, because anyone would have to
        say the words in order to process it, Andre announced,
                in his best imitation of the cable-TV investment advisor,

Pat, your car's been hit by a meteor. And it was true,
        confirmed by the police and the high school science teacher.
                Down the block a nightmare, if you want to think of it

that way, likewise the newspaper reporters and photographers
        another nightmare, of sorts: papers to sign,
                questions to answer as kids from the high school

pushed at each other and watched. Patty crumbled her cigarette
        in the pocket of the green hospital scrubs
                in which that morning she'd delivered

the unexpected news that a CAT scan was still clean,
        in which she'd pried open the fist of a man's
                irrefutable conviction that this should not be happening,

there should not be tubes running into his arms,
        other tubes running out from under his blanket.
                It's a nightmare, earth, where Heaven is when

near-disaster outraces disaster. Equally nightmare, if you want
        to think of it that way: that we can live in the face of this,
                as does the elderly couple Patty saw that morning

in the hospital gift shop,
        the woman no longer able to name the pink roses
                the man placed in her arms, folded her arms to hold.

As Patty spelled her name for a reporter, it struck her
      that everyone gathered on the corner of Elm and Pine
            was with her in a horror movie so bad it was good,

and a light that maybe was a camera-flash, and maybe not,
      made even the tall pierced kid
            who spat, and tapped a cigarette on his palm,

bobbing his head to some private tune, made even him
      look like a piece of Heaven fallen to this earth
            where Patty, as if out of the blue, saw

that had she quit smoking, as she'd been trying, for 53 days,
      she might have sat five minutes longer in her car,
            listening to the oldies station, craving nothing

but the part where Stevie Wonder sings, *that's why*
      I'll always be around, yeah, yeah, yeah, yeah,
            and Patty nodded and shivered and had to laugh

as she saw herself at the steering wheel, singing, as the meteor
      wheeled above Elm Street, no, Pine Street,
            yes, Pine.

RUNNING BACKWARDS

If the Nineties were aerobics and Eighties were jogging
and Seventies were hiking while stoned, the Sixties
were running backwards, every day,

at least at Endwell Elementary, one girl with leg braces
watching from the bleachers as we stood
backwards at the starting line, Mr. Rarick blowing his whistle

as we lurched from one end of the gym
to eventually the other. Why? It was a skill that would come in handy
if ever chased by a slow, rarely seen animal,

but why did we practice this drill
more than the other drills,
the fire, the air-raid?

Every day Mr. Rarick divided us into teams,
gave each team a baton, the demonstration of passing the baton.
It could not have been easy for him, either,

those mornings in the gym, watching us
wobble and tip and fall, some of us
falling over the fallen. We would almost

get the hang of it, when the school bell would ring,
and Cynthia, with the leg braces, braids tied with ribbon,
would join us in line, in the Sixties.

Each day was the day before: Cynthia
unlocking her braces so she could bend her legs and sit,
Mr. Rarick taking the whistle from his pocket,

lifting his clipboard and staring at it
as if it might tell him the future,
what he did not already know of the future.

We fell into place, shoulder to shoulder,
You are the future, he began.
You are America's future. And it was true,

each of us, and all of us together,
we could not help but be the future.
Time would carry us, most of us, forward,

whether we faced forward or back,
whether we glided gracefully or pumped our arms.
Time would take us into itself, into history,

where the same lessons must be learned
over and over, and nothing is new
except every day, like the day before it.

BEAUTY MARK

What is beauty? is a good question, but *What is a beauty mark?*
is equally good, with the added virtue of being answerable,

to a certain extent. A small brown dot, most usually
upon a woman's cheek or lip, it may be painted onto the skin

or pressed upon it, like a decal, and, I would guess,
over time there have been beauty-mark tattoos

for those most committed to it, or those most unwilling
to continually reapply it, those not attracted to caring

for the beauty mark, to keeping it like snuff in a ceramic box,
in a cool, dry place. But what is a beauty mark, beyond the physical?

Beauty is skin deep, but the beauty mark is deeper.
The picture of the devil is more frightening than the devil himself,

says the old Russian proverb. Beauty bedevils,
but the beauty mark bedevils beauty.

Beauty mark can mean freckle or mole, but usually
it is artifice, not nature, artifice exaggerated

so as not to be mistaken for nature. Jean Harlow, Miss Kitty,
Miss Peggy Lee, the woman behind the window

at the post office in Paris, who three times made the tall man
return to the table and reapply masking tape to his box,

each of these women bore a beauty mark through the day
as if she were a great ship sailing on the high seas,

a beauty mark meant--we can never know--to enhance
the skin's beauty or to conceal its imperfection,

each woman bearing it as if there were no higher calling
than to place on her changing face a small dot called beauty,

and carry it through the day, like a dark beacon
shining over the wild, the glittering water.

FOOD POEMS

I.

In the Russian orphanage, each night
the child is given a piece of bread
to hold in her hands while she sleeps,
so she knows that tomorrow she will eat.

II.

In a village outside of Addis Ababa,
one child gives another a banana.
The second child peels it, returns the fruit,
eats the peel.

III.

On Yom Kippur, Avenue of the Americas,
a woman hands the homeless man a sandwich,
which he refuses, saying, *No thank you.
Today I'm fasting.*

IV.

The parent is becoming a child.
Mother of God, feed those who will feed her.

Holy Mother, rest your arm across her shoulders,
your other arm behind her knees.
Lift her like a child being carried to bed
in a world where children are carried to bed.

SOUTHERN ITALIAN CUISINE COOKING CLASS: STUFFED ARTICHOKE

Who likes to use a knife clumsily,
and with others watching?

Who likes to feel ire rise for the nice woman
whistling as she dices shallots?

> *Cut off the base of the artichoke*
> *so it sits like a woody teacup.*
> *Trim the tip of each resistant leaf.*
> *Tease each leaf outward, and into each pocket*
> *spoon seasoned breadcrumbs.*

Who wants to face additional direction?

> *Set stuffed artichoke in pan already containing stuffed artichokes*
> *of all of the other cooking class students.*
> *Steam for one hour.*

Who likes to spend an hour-and-a-half
for the effort-filled pleasure of stuffed artichoke,
teeth raking each inedible leaf?

Who believes we are required to love everything?

Who believes we are required to labor with love,
or even with engagement?

Who likes to feel lazy, ungrateful?

Who can't come to hate even the simplest
of ingredients: sea salt, lemon,
intractable quarter-moons of garlic?

Stuffed Artichoke, armored assassin of time,
spiky indictment of impatience,

of inability
to sink into the moment,
to willingly get one's hands dirty,

Artichoke,
who likes to learn from a vegetable?

RING

Rose gold engraved with a grain of wheat,
      neither large nor small, hard to say

if it belonged to the man or the woman,
      before the child that came of that union,

then the child's child, and how many times again,
      lives brief as grass, as wheat,

but the ring survives, shining today
      from the glass case in the rare book shop,

as if readers strapped for cash traded
      circle pins and tie tacks for the missing volume,

for a second copy of the book they could not give away.
      Hard to say how many of us

who live most deeply in books
      have asked to see the ring, meaning to touch it, slip it on

as if marrying ourselves to the moment,
      pledging ourselves to this slant light

of an afternoon in late August,
      the faint hum of trucks on the interstate

that used to be fields, back when August meant
      the lull before harvest, the rare afternoon

for sitting at the table after the pie is gone,
      looking across the plates at your partner

and allowing that life's worst days brought you somehow
      here. There. Easy to marry ourselves to the moment

but hard to be faithful to it, even as we set the ring
      on our palm, check inside for inscriptions,

find no names, no dates,
     just a white tag, *$100*, a steal

if a hundred dollars weren't a hundred dollars,
     if it were the ring we wanted

and not the ring's shining,
     not the ring's catching our eye,

just catching it,
     grain of wheat married briefly to light.

MR. BENTLEY

You made us dissect a worm and then a frog.
You were skinny. Your hair was greasy.
You were our last class of the day, until that day

the English teacher stood in your place
and told us to open our books, read for the hour.
That evening after dinner, our fathers,

newspaper crackling in their laps, would ask,
Isn't your teacher named Bentley?
A police officer had discovered your apartment

contained stolen goods: silverware, jewelry,
priceless antiques, whatever that meant.
New in town, you'd get invited to dinner

and steal a silver box, a clock,
a vase so familiar as to be invisible.
You stole a pair of andirons.

The next day at lunch we laughed, joking
how could you steal anything with those scrawny arms,
with one hand always pushing up your glasses?

It was mid-June. Most of your work was done,
was keeping us quiet as spring drove our bodies wild.
You wore white socks. Your pants were short.

Whenever people welcomed you,
asked you to sit at their table, to eat,
some place inside of you asked to be filled

and you had to take something from that home
to call your own. Mr. Bentley, the newspaper said
you did not sell what you stole, every missing thing

found on the floor at the foot of your bed.
You would always say *like so.*
You pin the frog's legs like so.

You place the blade like so.
Like so, your life was opened and spread
and that place inside of you

that sprang to life at the table
over pot roast and coffee and stories,
that place became something we could not say,

became a silence in the middle of our laughter.
Mr. Bentley, you made us look at the inside of things,
see what made them live, or at least

kept them alive for their short time.
You let us choose the worm, the frog.
You let us name it.

CALL IT

They were so poor the man lay in his casket
in the only good luck he'd ever had: a $5,000

Harris tweed hound's-tooth-check suit his ex-wife
had found, perfect condition, in a junk shop,

a good-enough story even before you know
the seat of his pants is missing,

the fully-lined, knife-pleated pant-legs
sheared clean off at his knees,

the back of his suit coat cut away,
and his ex-wife kneeling at his side

in a Harris tweed hound's-tooth-check dress,
the two of them like a couple on vacation

in matching Hawaiian shirts, although
instead of a map he holds, sort of, a prayer book.

Call it a final joke between them for old times' sake,
or call it her revenge for years that cannot be lived again

except in memories, most of them bad memories,
but some so sweet she is in mortal danger

of forgiving everything. Call it, finally, something
no one outside the two of them can ever understand,

nor even they themselves, clothed in the cast off,
the found, the ruined, the made new.

Freud's Little Statues

He liked to hold them and offer them to his patients to hold.
—ArtNews, *Summer 2007*

The father of psychotherapy, mourning his father's death,
          frequented the antique shops of Vienna, full
                    of stone angels and bronze girls playing flutes.

He wandered among nameless terracotta gods
          worn to nubbins by worship or neglect, say,
                    set in a garden and then forgotten

as the plants grew up around them.
          From 1896, the year of his father's death,
                    until 1938, when he fled Vienna for London,

Freud often returned from his afternoon walk
          with a little statue, assembling in his room
                    a small heaven. Here, he wrote

The Interpretation of Dreams, reading passages aloud
          to the audience crowded onto shelves, and tables,
                    and along the edge of his desk,

where the figures served as paperweights.
          The father of talk therapy would lie on the couch,
                    wishing he could talk to his father, about the weather,

dinner last night followed by a cigar, just a cigar.
          Without his saying a word, the statues understood.
                    Statues are experts on loneliness,

for they are made by someone
          who works quietly, alone.
                    They are good travel companions.

Many of Freud's statues accompanied him
          on vacation, luxuriating in a seaside room
                    before returning home, to help

patients on their most difficult journeys
       by doing nothing more than being
              handed from doctor to patient,

and, finally, back again—
       stone wings in brief flight,
              brief hands on wings.

ASKING FOR BREAKFAST

One should live each day with the confidence
I displayed that day in Paris, when, at 4 PM,
I said to the waiter, *We would like to eat*

breakfast, if you please, exceedingly proud
of my accent, eager to demonstrate it again
for the white-haired waiter who raised

his dark eyebrows, requested I *répétez*.
He looked at my husband, then back at me,
and I like to think the waiter thought

I was boasting of our sex life, was suggesting
we had spent the day in bed, and not just
any day, but a day in Paris—

vendors polishing cages in the bird market
behind Notre Dame, shopkeepers in long aprons
washing sidewalks, well-dressed bureaucrats

riding bicycles, bouquets of flowers balanced
across the handlebars, as if they were in love
with the work ahead—that day, in bed.

I like to think we rose in the waiter's esteem,
two Americans alive to the pleasures of the body,
and able to convey this information

with a sentence, although simple, stunningly
Gallic in subtlety: breakfast at the hour for tea.
But that day in Paris I thought not a whit

of the waiter's thought, not even as I caught
my mistake, and laughed, caught
my husband's amused, affectionate eyes.

That day in Paris, I gave not a flit of a thought
to the lonely table imagination sets. Hungry,
I asked for breakfast. I asked again.

HAND

after Kafka's "The Hunger Artist"

My sister and I led the hunger artist out of his cage,
but I suspect you do not remember me,
for she fell to crying, was led away as the crowd jeered,

while I stood quietly, holding the hunger artist's hand,
small bundle of knuckles, as the record states.
An identified girl replaced my vivid sister,

and the three of us walked to the table
where he, to his despair, ate, sick
to be robbed of knowing how long he could fast,

but our town, forgive me, one brief course
in the banquet of his career.
When years later I heard he'd finally starved—

he'd said *for want of food which I enjoyed*—
I, once again unlike my sister, did not know what I felt,
not beyond, again, the physical. I was at work,

in my studio, my hands wet, clay-stained,
guiding the gray slab up and outward
such that it might become a cup or bowl.

As the messenger watched, I kept working:
in the hands a balance of strength and delicacy,
in the gut and down the leg a steady beat

to keep the pedal, the wheel, moving.
I watched the dark space open inside the clay
and then I decided to deepen it, to tip

the vessel's edge into a lip,
to fashion a small and shapely handle,
the better to raise this darkness, and drink.

I mean not the darkness of sorrow, of lonely compulsion,
nor the darkness at the heart of all creation.
I mean this literal darkness,

the one the hunger artist still feasted upon
as the crowd roared and my sister reeled
and I, hollow, stood fast, and felt his hand tighten

so weakly I could have imagined it. Then,
he squeezed my hand again, as if he were my true sister,
or my self, which in those days I did not yet know.

I was young and now I am old.
My hand still hungers for his hand,
which some days I find inside of this clay.

I know I should weep for him
but only my hands weep,
and they are full of joy.

INTO THE NIGHT

for David Sanjek, 1952-2011

Do you have good light? Good kitchen knives?
A fish market? A Thai restaurant like the one
on Olive Boulevard, with yellow Formica counters,

an *endless cup* of tea, poured as you walk in?
Were your hundreds of CDs and books
already up there? Unpacked, and shelved?

Are your parents there?
Are they young? Is there time, up there?
I don't mean enough time. I mean time.

Didn't we talk late into the night? Remember,
If there were no time, could there be music?
There is music up there, right? New music,

by someone nobody's yet heard of?
Definitely "Autumn Leaves," by Mr. Julian
"Cannonball" Adderley, "I'm In the Mood

for Love," by King Pleasure and Blossom Dearie?
Have you met Ray Charles? Is he still blind?
Have you met Milton? Ditto.

Do you still wear rimless, thick-lensed glasses?
Do you wear the Greek fisherman's cap
you left on the train, circa 1987?

Do you know that I wanted to burn your baseball cap?
That I hated, sometimes, your capacity
to retain every fact you had ever learned,

no matter how arcane, refined, popular, or just
plain weird? That I did not always want to know
how the scene was shot, the special effect produced,

or the sauce was made? Do you know
that when you held the spoon to your lips, and
slowly named the ingredients, you taught how to live?

Remember the Friday night radio program
that ended with Ben Webster's "Chelsea Bridge,"
with the DJ who called himself *The Man in the Red Vest?*

Have you met him? You may expect me to ask
if he wears a red vest, but I don't want to know.
I want to know, has he asked you for a playlist?

Have you scribbled for him, on a paper napkin,
a column of the songs you love, and
a column of the songs you almost love, because

you love the deep tenderness that resides in the flaws?
As your new friend read the list, did you
stare at him over the top of your glasses

as you would stare at me, as the movie's final credits
scrolled, and the screen went black,
the house lights rose?

Can you believe that I have never stopped using
your single-word charm for avoiding the long good-bye,
to which we both are given, *okseeyoubye?*

After the movie, you would look at me
and lean slightly away, so as to see me more clearly,
and then you would ask, *Well? What do you think?*

I think you do not know
that I have never forgotten, from the late 1970s,
your brief, unfortunate penchant

for cheap Hawaiian shirts,
that I think those shirts the sole instance
of your loving anything lightly, and not forever.

LIVING LARGE

for Denise Duhamel and the Ultra-Talk Poets,
which sounds like a 1980s garage band
but, to my knowledge, is not

How often do I stay at the New York Hilton?
When do I get the chance to approach the Hilton's Theater Desk and ask
anything? So I ask the nice man in dark navy if there is one seat for the opera
tonight, and then I get to experience myself, well, sort of myself,
standing just off the lobby in the Hilton, saying, *The Metropolitan,*
saying, when he asks which opera, *Manon,* just
as an uncommonly tall couple follow their luggage past me
and their life seems no better than mine. I don't know a lot about opera,
but I love it, and yet I am secretly relieved when the Theater Man tells me
that the house is full, for, in truth, I am tired from a day full of poetry and poets.
What I want most is to go up to my room and lie on the bed,
put on the heavy bathrobe, pull back the comforter and prop myself
on the ridiculous surfeit of exquisite pillows. *Thank you,* I say as I turn
from the Theater Desk, which sounds as though it is a stage prop, not a real desk,
as if it is made of cardboard or scrap wood, two-dimensional,
like the street on *Gunsmoke,* where the buildings were flat panels
painted to look like the saloon, the general store, et cetera, a plywood Dodge City.
Since the actors were trained professionals, they didn't need the building to be real.
It was real in their minds, and that was enough, for all of us,
the show running for something like 20 years. Every actor got rich
as a bank robber. I have often wondered, why did the stagecoach wheels
always seem to turn backwards? If you know why, please contact me.
I'm in Room 3402, even though I ask myself, *am I making the best use*
of my time in New York? in general? I might ask, but this question is not real.
I already know the answer, and it is *No.* Living is not my gift,
not the living that is large, and lasts into the night. Even traveling home
tomorrow on the train, I will not be the one who slips off my coat and gets comfortable,
sips from a cup of coffee bought especially for the trip.
I will be the one riding in the overheated car with my coat on,
afraid that if I remove my coat I will leave it behind,
that if I close my eyes I will sleep through my stop.
I cannot stay awake late at night, although my mother was a night owl,
still is, although her day and her night now blend slowly together.
When I was a child, she would sit up late waiting for my father

to come home from work. I would hear her stir sugar into her coffee
as she watched TV or, finally, read the newspaper.
Time is, of course, the greatest luxury, because there is so little time,
and so little real knowledge of how best to use it. Sure, writing poems,
making art. seems worthwhile, as good a way as any to love
what is slipping away, to slip oneself into time as one slips into the thick
terry robe that would convince one that one knows how to live, to really live,
alive in every cell of one's body and not just mainly in one's head.
As the elevator doors close behind me, I remember reading
that on *Bonanza*, my other favorite show, the exteriors and the interiors
were shot on different sets, so you'd knock on a door and then
you'd be driven to another set, where you could enter. The inside
and the outside did not connect. How real is that? In my experience,
very. The Ponderosa is still my idea of luxury, with its stone fireplace
as large as my first apartment, not that I cannot also appreciate
my plush room at the Hilton, not that I don't still, sort of, wish
I were dressing for the opera instead of opening the drawer
of the bedside table and finding Conrad Hilton's 1957
autobiography, *Be My Guest*, the 1994 Fireside Press paperback edition,
288 pages curled by ten-plus years of guests sitting on the toilet
in a steam-filled bathroom. The book does not lie flat anymore.
Without opening it I can read the table of contents, the first chapter
You've Got to Dream, the last chapter *There Is an Art to Living*,
which I guess is the chapter about poetry.
In many obituaries I've noticed that so-and-so *wrote poetry*. Scientists
and chess masters and prima ballerinas and people who used to be
child actors, they all wrote poetry. When I was younger
I used to chafe at this, even smirk. Then I went through a stage
where I thought it sweet, like collecting glass animals or
knitting with big needles. But now the part about poetry
is the part I hardly read. I consider it the given part, as poetry itself is given,
or not. If I had gone to the opera, which is to say, if there had been one
cheap seat to be had and I had had the energy to walk the eight blocks
uptown, I would now, from a spot high and far, like a fly ball, be staring
as a singer the size of my thumb releases a voice larger than life,
larger even than a large life, although I wonder why *large life*
sounds smaller than just plain *life*. But I am too tired to think.

Instead, I thumb through *Be My Guest*. The last page reads,
What I like about prayer is that it is a means of communication with God.
You can speak to Him any time, night or day, and you can know
with certainty that He is listening to you. Contact with God makes us
successes in living. Once I would have smirked. Once I would never
have committed this to writing, any of this. I close the book,
which is when I notice that, in the drawing on the yellow and blue cover,
Conrad Hilton seems to lean forward. His towering hotel seems
to spring out of his head, but it also looks as if the hotel
has brained him, and Hilton falls forward while his pale blue eyes look upward,
which is a gift, looking upward. Hilton believes
that if he just opens his mouth, God will listen, and that God listens
even if we do not speak at all. Hilton believes that God,
in some large and well-appointed room in the sky, waits
for us to speak, but that it is also OK with God
if we do not speak at all, hard as this is to believe.

Let Me Reach for Outrageous Comparison

say, between a homemade watercolor paper doll
        made in Owego, New York circa 1830
                and Rembrandt's 1655 portrait of his wife Hendrickje

as she wades into a moonlit river to bathe.
        Both figures are female. Each wears a white shift.
            The paper doll's torso is thin,

thin arms held away from her body
        in accordance with the conventions of paper dolls.
            Hendrickje's body is full, calves and forearms round

as she lifts the hem of her shift as far as her thighs,
        in accordance with the conventions of 17th-century bathers
            and of 17th-century paintings of bathers,

although Hendrickje's right hand bursts through convention,
        her right hand a crude gray smear,
            a lumpish square with two slash-marks

holding up the finely scored linen.
        The paper doll's hands, both of them, also are crude.
            They are each shapeless, merely an end to the arm,

as if whoever painted the doll had grown tired,
        or the candle by which she worked
            burned low, sputtered out.

Art critics conjecture that Rembrandt first painted
        Hendrickje's right hand in all of its intricacy
            and then he painted over it, the perfect hand

covered by a rough gray sack
        which Rembrandt worked hastily, his brush muddy
            with all of the colors in the painting,

his brushstrokes wild with all he had ever seen,
        horses, pigs, dye-vats, looms, kid gloves, lace.
            Into the sack he throws tobacco, cabbages, ale,

canals and all that floats in them, all that surfaces,
      also into the sack a boat weathered and docked,
            which Rembrandt finds as he paints,

the boat the act of painting,
      of seeing what he did not know
            there was to see,

the boat into which Rembrandt then climbs,
      moonlit-scrolled water quivering with his weight
            as it quivers around Hendrickje's left ankle

as she wades farther in.
      Quivering at the hem of the doll's shift,
            in blue pencil, is the name *Polly*.

It is unclear whether Polly is the doll or the painter, perhaps
      the painter's frail daughter or sister, who is a light so brief, so light,
            on the slightest breeze it leaves, a leaf on water.

The doll's feet disappear, as do Hendrickje's, into blackness,
      albeit into shoes, shoes of black crayon pressed so thickly
            the black slickens, shines with light.

Let me reach: The paper doll's shoes
      shine with the light of Hendrickje's bathing.
            Let me reach: One light touches everything.

One light touches everything, as does one darkness.
      And the dark and the light bathe each other.
            Let me reach: there is nothing

for which light will not find correspondence.
      There is nothing that darkness will not claim,
            not the shoe of the doll, not the image of moonlight

nor moonlight itself, nor Rembrandt,
      not even though he steps into the boat
            and unties the rope holding the boat to shore

so the boat can drift like a leaf on water, out,
        beyond Hendrickje and the gray sack she carries,
                the light, the shimmer and shadow she carries

in her eyes and hair and shoulders,
        the light she carries because there is no choice,
                is there? It is all one cloth.

Light laps the hem of darkness, darkness
        the hem of light. It is all one cloth.
                Hendrickje and the paper doll, their white shifts,

are cut of this cloth.
        But that is too easy, isn't it,
                to say that what touches joins?

Let me reach with Hendrickje's ruined hand,
        the one that carries the gray sack,
                and also with her other, beautiful hand,

and let me reach with both
        of the paper doll's hands, so crude
                they also are delicate, alive

with the effort it took to dare them.
        Let me reach with these hands.
                Let me reach with these hands, out.

ENDNOTES

"Cheese-of-the-Month Club" is for Jo Ann Clark.

"Exercises from *The Manual of Proper Correspondence*" is a found poem.

"Lament" is based upon Cleve Gray's installation entitled "Threnody," which was produced for the Neuberger Museum in 1972-73. A meditation on life and death produced in protest of the war in Vietnam, "Threnody" is a fourteen-panel oil painting that covers the four walls of a large gallery. Each panel suggests a dancing figure meant to evoke, in Gray's words, "the dance of life and death."

"Denise Poiret" is about the wife of the fashion designer Paul Poiret. Her bright and fanciful style, influenced by folk costume and modern art, inspired many of her husband's designs.

"Living Large" is indebted to poet David Graham, whose essay "The Ultra-Talk Poem and Mark Halliday" originally appeared in *Valparaiso Review*. The essay defines and delights in *ultra-talk* poetry (the term coined by Halliday in a review of David Kirby's poetry), and considers various practitioners of it, contemporary and classic.

"The Navigator" is for Ralph Langley.

Suzanne Cleary was born in Binghamton, New York. Winner of a Pushcart Prize, her poems have appeared in journals including *Poetry London* and *The Atlantic*, and in anthologies including *Best American Poetry*. Her previous books are *Keeping Time* (2002) and *Trick Pear* (2007). Professor of English at the State University of New York at Rockland, she also teaches as core faculty of the MFA in Creative Writing program of Converse College.